Getting Ready *for* Revival

"Go home....
Lock yourself in your room....
Kneel down in the middle of the
floor and with a piece of chalk,
draw a circle round yourself....
There, on your knees, pray fervently
and brokenly, that God would start
a Revival within that chalk circle!"
– Gypsy Smith

Stuart D. Reynolds

Foreword by Rev. Richard Reed

WESTBOW
PRESS®
A DIVISION OF THOMAS NELSON
& ZONDERVAN

This book is a work of non-fiction. Unless otherwise noted, the author and the publisher make no explicit guarantees as to the accuracy of the information contained in this book and in some cases, names of people and places have been altered to protect their privacy.

All Scripture quotations, unless otherwise indicated, are taken from the Holy Bible, New International Version®, NIV®. Copyright ©1973, 1978, 1984, 2011 by Biblica, Inc.™ Used by permission of Zondervan. All rights reserved worldwide. www.zondervan.com The "NIV" and "New International Version" are trademarks registered in the United States Patent and Trademark Office by Biblica, Inc.™

Scripture taken from the King James Version of the Bible.

Scripture quotations marked MSG are taken from THE MESSAGE, copyright © 1993, 1994, 1995, 1996, 2000, 2001, 2002 by Eugene H. Peterson. Used by permission of NavPress. All rights reserved. Represented by Tyndale House Publishers, Inc.

WestBow Press books may be ordered through booksellers or by contacting:

WestBow Press
A Division of Thomas Nelson & Zondervan
1663 Liberty Drive
Bloomington, IN 47403
www.westbowpress.com
1 (866) 928-1240

Because of the dynamic nature of the Internet, any web addresses or links contained in this book may have changed since publication and may no longer be valid. The views expressed in this work are solely those of the author and do not necessarily reflect the views of the publisher, and the publisher hereby disclaims any responsibility for them.

Any people depicted in stock imagery provided by Thinkstock are models, and such images are being used for illustrative purposes only. Certain stock imagery © Thinkstock.

ISBN: 978-1-9736-1344-2 (sc)
ISBN: 978-1-9736-1345-9 (e)

Library of Congress Control Number: 2018900283

Print information available on the last page.

WestBow Press rev. date: 1/11/2018

Contents

This book is dedicated to my wife, Helen, and daughters, Heather and Leah, the finest Christ-Ones I know. Steadfast in love, courageous in faith, and partners in the gospel.

"I had fainted, unless I had believed to see the goodness of the LORD in the land of the living."
(Psalm 27:13 KJV)

I would also like to thank my friend and mentor, Rev. Richard Reed, for agreeing to pen the foreword to this book, and for his unstinting support and protection of me and mine. In 1 Chronicles 12:32, the Bible speaks of the "children of Issachar... men that had understanding of the times, to know what Israel ought to do" (KJV). In this generation, Brother Reed is among their number.

Foreword

Everyone will profit in a number of ways by asking three questions:

1) Where am I going with my life?
2) What have I done of eternal value thus far?
3) How can I best impact my world with the time I have left?

This is a book for those who sincerely desire to make a difference in the lives of others. The key is that it speaks directly and specifically to the heart and to the problems which plague many of today's modern churches. *Getting Ready for Revival* will help answer all three of the previously listed questions and prepare the reader for a more spiritually productive life. A personal, prayerful, and careful study of this book and the piercing statements which are made will add value to the life of those who are hungry for all God has to give.

I have known Stuart Reynolds for eighteen years and have followed his ministry both in the UK and the USA, especially his revival meetings. I have attended more than fifty of his revival services in Tennessee. We have travelled together in preparation for revival meetings across portions of Tennessee, and I have had the privilege of hosting Stuart and his family in our home on several occasions. I have also enjoyed the hospitality of the Reynolds family, having stayed many nights as their guest during their ministry in England

and Ireland. I praise God for the friendship of Stuart, Helen, Heather, and Leah that has enriched my spiritual life and helped me make a difference in my world. During my extended times with Stuart, I have found him to be a man of God, an excellent expository preacher, and a colleague in ministry who has "endured (life's trials) as seeing Him who is invisible."

I recommend this book as a preparation guide, not only for a series of revival services, but most of all as a spiritual stimulus for giving God your best during the time you have yet to live. I also highly recommend Stuart as an evangelist for your church for a series of revival services. I have used him during my pastorates in Iowa and in Tennessee and found his singing and preaching ministry to be appreciated by our people and his pulpit ministry to be productive with seekers both among the saints and those seeking salvation.

Pastor Richard Reed
Church of the Nazarene
Pastoral Care Ministry
East Tennessee District
Tullahoma, Tennessee

Introduction

After *The Broken Pastor*, I never thought I would write another book, much less one on revival. In the 1989 film *Field of Dreams*, Kevin Costner's character keeps hearing a voice, which no one else could hear, urging him, "If you build it, he will come." This book has been borne by a similar compulsion. However, it's not so much a dream as a burden. Neither is it from inward but from upward: "If you write it, some will read it." You are the fruit and proof of that and the answer to much prayer.

I am not an expert in revival; I am a seeker after God. Such is not a boast but a confession. I am not the only one who is distressed at what is being allowed to happen in the church and desperate to see God move in revival in the remaining time He has allotted me and you before heaven. There are certainly other books you could be reading and perhaps other themes you would rather read about. Better books have been written about revival, but I would suggest no other truth is more needed today in the life of the church and the community of God's people than that of revival. If this offering can help contribute to a conversation that has for too long been silent, then its purpose will be achieved and the prayer behind it answered.

> LORD, thou hast been favourable unto thy land:
> thou hast brought back the captivity of Jacob. Thou

hast forgiven the iniquity of thy people, thou hast covered all their sin. Selah.

Thou hast taken away all thy wrath: thou hast turned thyself from the fierceness of thine anger.

Turn us, O God of our salvation, and cause thine anger toward us to cease.

Wilt thou be angry with us for ever? wilt thou draw out thine anger to all generations? Wilt thou not revive us again: that thy people may rejoice in thee?

Shew us thy mercy, O LORD, and grant us thy salvation.

I will hear what God the LORD will speak: for he will speak peace unto his people, and to his saints: but let them not turn again to folly.

Surely his salvation is nigh them that fear him; that glory may dwell in our land. Mercy and truth are met together; righteousness and peace have kissed each other.

Truth shall spring out of the earth; and righteousness shall look down from heaven. Yea, the LORD shall give that which is good; and our land shall yield her increase.

Righteousness shall go before him; and shall set us in the way of his steps.

(Psalm 85 KJV)

1

Realisation

"See, I have this day set thee over the nations and over the kingdoms, to root out, and to pull down, and to destroy, and to throw down, to build and to plant."
(Jeremiah 1:10 KJV)

In his 1937 book, *The Church Must First Repent*, J Edwin Orr noted that of God's six-fold commission to Jeremiah, only two are positive, whilst the other four are negative. His contention being that a destructive ministry is needed before there can ever be a constructive ministry. Orr commented:

> The glorious message of the position of every believer
> in Christ is a comfort to many souls. But it cannot
> bring much blessing to a stubborn Christian living
> in disobedience and conscious sin. He needs to act
> on the teaching of repentance and confession and

1

cleansing first, and then he may comfort himself with other truths.[1]

How many have just enough of the world to be uncomfortable in the church and just enough of the church to be uncomfortable in the world? What a terrible predicament. We cannot be living in negligence and conscious disobedience to God and at the same time be at peace in His presence amongst His gathered people, not to mention being in a position of close abiding in personal God awareness from day to day. Orr continued:

> Positional truth cannot be profitably taught until conditional teaching has had its effect. Cast no pearls before swine. So great is this problem, that when the preacher hits out against sin among believers and urges purity of life, critics cry "Navel-gazing," and some insist that he is trying to divert the eyes of the people away from Christ towards self and shortcomings.... Let us comfort one another with the grand truths of our position in Christ. But let us not make excuse by saying that our "completeness in Him" permits us to wink at known sin.[2]

What a crucially relevant and timeless insight. Revival, by definition and consequence, testifies to a need, a lack, something to be removed: *"destruction,"* that what remains may be corrected and properly restored and even replaced: *"construction."* We live in a Church-day, with our prevailing "Kingdom Now," "Latter Rain," "Emerging Church," and "New Apostolic Reformation" theology which sound out and allow only positive vibes and images about the state of the church today and its fate tomorrow, no matter, and seemingly without loss and without cross. In so much, church life has forsaken the altar of sacrifice and the pulpit of proclamation for a stage where we are continually watching and endorsing and applauding ourselves. While the rest of the world is going to hell, we have circled the wagons waiting for Jesus to come; in the meantime, just having endless services and events for ourselves, as we gorge on our self-acclaimed "slickness" and "cleverness" of how well we are doing and how good we are. Much of what is passed off and accepted as Christian worship – not to mention Christ living – is froth not faith, mush and gush without truth and grace, because it is driven by emotion, dominated by music, drenched in fleshly sentiment. Not Christ-centred, neither Bible based, and thus impossible to be Holy Spirit graced, guided, and guarded to the glory of God. The Bible counsels, and indeed warns, us in Philippians 3:3 to put "no confidence in the flesh" (KJV). Yet, that is exactly what we see promoted and paraded, as we see ourselves further descend in many places from mindless worship to messy church.

To question the status quo of what has become our norm is to be labelled as "negative … traditional … legalistic … condemning … quenching the Holy Spirit." With the exception of where many go on a Sunday morning, much of Christian profession and lifestyle is no longer distinct from that of our pagan neighbours. Yet it must not be challenged, as Jesus my "personal" Saviour has become Jesus my "private" Saviour. Scriptural preachers are forced out of the local church, as those in rebellion before God are affirmed and allowed to remain, even those living in conscious disobedience.

Ezekiel's Bad Dream (Ezekiel 8:1–18 The Message):

> In the sixth year, in the sixth month and the fifth day, while I was sitting at home meeting with the leaders of Judah, it happened that the hand of my Master, GOD, gripped me. When I looked, I was astonished. What I saw looked like a man—from the waist down like fire and from the waist up like highly burnished bronze. He reached out what

looked like a hand and grabbed me by the hair. The Spirit swept me high in the air and carried me in visions of God to Jerusalem, to the entrance of the north gate of the Temple's inside court where the image of the sex goddess that makes God so angry had been set up. Right before me was the Glory of the God of Israel, exactly like the vision I had seen out on the plain.

He said to me, "Son of man, look north." I looked north and saw it: Just north of the entrance loomed the altar of the sex goddess, Asherah, that makes God so angry. Then he said, "Son of man, do you see what they're doing? Outrageous obscenities! And doing them right here! It's enough to drive Me right out of My own Temple. But you're going to see worse yet."

He brought me to the door of the Temple court. I looked and saw a gaping hole in the wall. He said, "Son of man, dig through the wall." I dug through the wall and came upon a door. He said, "Now walk through the door and take a look at the obscenities they're engaging in."

I entered and looked. I couldn't believe my eyes: Painted all over the walls were pictures of reptiles and animals and monsters—the whole pantheon of Egyptian gods and goddesses—being worshiped by Israel. In the middle of the room were seventy of the leaders of Israel, with Jaazaniah son of Shaphan standing in the middle. Each held his censer with the incense rising in a fragrant cloud. He said, 'Son of man, do you see what the elders are doing here in the dark, each one before his favourite god-picture? They tell themselves, "GOD doesn't see us. GOD has forsaken the country."

Then he said, "You're going to see worse yet."

He took me to the entrance at the north gate of the Temple of GOD. I saw women sitting there, weeping for Tammuz, the Babylonian fertility god. He said, "Have you gotten an eyeful, son of man? You're going to see worse yet."

Finally, he took me to the inside court of the Temple of GOD. There between the porch and the altar were about twenty-five men. Their backs were to GOD's Temple. They were facing east, bowing in worship to the sun.

He said, "Have you seen enough, son of man? Isn't it bad enough that Judah engages in these outrageous obscenities? They fill the country with violence and now provoke Me even further with their obscene gestures. That's it. They have an angry God on their hands! From now on, no mercy. They can shout all they want, but I'm not listening."

A report of carnality ... idolatry ... and anarchy – we already know it's in the world ... but in the church?

Ezekiel's Nightmare: Our Now

Like never before, in the church, this is what is to be seen:

- Carnality amongst the worshippers.

- The cult of personality amongst the priests as servants become ornaments.
- A corrupted holy community.
- A religion marked by egotism, marred by indulgence, and shrouded in vagueness, but devoid of consecration, self-denial, and the distinctive clarity of purity.
- The Lord's Day has become for the majority the Lord's "half-day" (or even less).
- Biblical ignorance abounds, as does its consequence of spiritual impotence.
- Confrontation and condemnation of sin has been removed from our vocabulary in favour of the mantra that endlessly affirms, despite sin … as sin is redefined and excused, allowed to remain under other names and guises, but never removed.
- Pastors have become managers, no longer shepherds and preachers, but life-coaches with worldly self-help messages, no longer prophets with the Word from God.
- The absence of accountability.
- The absence of holiness.
- The absence of the supernatural as many professing Christ-Ones in the lives they live and the churches they attend do not need God to be and do.
- The absence of God in our midst.

Our nightmare, our now. As never before, not because we are better or worse than those of Ezekiel's time, but because of where and when we live:

- in the light of the Christ's Incarnation,
- on the other side of the Cross in His Resurrection,
- after the unreserved giving of the Holy Spirit at Pentecost to reside in every Christ-One,
- within the established church/Body of Christ,

- having God's Book, the Bible, the complete and finished canon of God's written and living revelation of Himself in truth.

Truly, we are of that generation Jesus spoke of when He said of John the Baptist: "He that is least in the kingdom of heaven is greater than he" (Matthew 11:11 KJV); all we see ... all we know ... all we possess ... all we have been covered by and trusted with, holding in our grasp, and yet being a modern-day "Samson" who, for all our heritage and strength and promise and calling and experience, found and exposed, lounging in the lap of Delilah, presuming we know it all, when all the time, not knowing that "the LORD [has] departed from [us]" (see Judges 16:20 KJV).

In the pew, there are those who are rightly troubled, not only by what is being seen, but also over what is not being heard from the pulpit (if a pulpit still remains). Many pastors are intimidated – afraid of their congregations. It's not that these preachers are saying anything wrong but that they are just not saying enough. In *Feeding Sheep or Amusing Goats*, C. H. Spurgeon contended,

> From speaking out as the Puritans did, the Church has gradually toned down her testimony, then winked at and excused the frivolities of the day. Then she tolerated them in her borders. Now she has adopted them under the plea of reaching the masses.... The need of the hour for today's ministry is believing scholarship joined with earnest spirituality, the one springing from the other as fruit from the root. The need is Biblical doctrine, so understood and felt, that it sets men on fire.[3]

Are we not increasingly dismayed at what our children and grandchildren have never known in their experience of God in His church?

- The sense of the sacred, not just the singing of songs.
- A moving and working of God which is neither manipulated nor forced by the antics and methods of whatever is doing the rounds of the latest and newest, no matter how theologically inept and scripturally unsupportable, in it not being the "truest."
- Strong biblical preaching that speaks of the eternal in addressing the soul, not just caressing the flesh with silly jokes, sentimental stories, contrived videos – and all in a neat fifteen-minute segment – which amuse and even move to tears, piquing our interests, without ever piercing our hearts and changing us for better and for ever, in the confrontation with truth that cannot leave us the same, for better or for worse.

From Fall-Out to Bail-Out via Every "Out" in Between

The fall-out rate amongst churchgoers who have never been Christ-Ones is alarming, because of what the church has largely sold out to: short-term solutions which are so shallow and untested, which within a matter of a few years are quickly grown out of and left behind, because as we get older, life becomes more complicated, and we discover that we need something more than the religious make-believe so much of our modern worship songs are. Just as the world is dominated and driven by entertainment, so the church has become overrun and overruled by songwriters and worship-artists, setting the tone of how we now worship, having laid the tracks of what we now believe.

Our doctrines and disciplines have been shelved and are now shaped by our musicians and the trends of their branded music, no longer preserved and passed on by our Bible teachers or church traditions on the foundation of the timeless Word of God. This church generation – shared by people of all ages – has to be one of the most arrogant in what we suppose we can now ditch because of what we assume about ourselves that we, in this moment, have got it all together in a way that those before us just did not, and so we can jettison two thousand years of church doctrine, practice, and tradition, in favour of our own – even the tradition of having no traditions, the practice of having no form, and the doctrine of holding to none.

Much of modern-day Western Christianity is nothing more than religious humanism, seeking fleshly answers to spiritual questions, offering worldly wisdom in the face of eternal needs – centred around and promoting and pampering self, further evidenced by the ever-popular prosperity teachers who tell us that God is primarily concerned for our personal enhancement and advancement, in the ever-widening context of what is called Emerging Church, where truth is no longer absolute and thus the Bible no longer trustworthy as the authoritative, unchanging, unerring Word of God. Is there not something amiss where the true mark of spirituality is deemed to be how ridiculous we can be for God and not how radical, with holiness dumbed-down and drowned out by the clumsy clanging of hollowness? In the fullness of time, what we in our "wisdom" have thrown out will be the very same over which the apostates bail out.

In the words of the wise preacher, "There is no new thing under the sun" (Ecclesiastes 1:9 KJV). The world has always been pagan – without God – but amongst God's people, even as early as Exodus, on the heels of deliverance from Egypt, we see God's people having "fashioned" (Exodus 32:4 KJV) by themselves for themselves a golden calf, which they still referred to as "the LORD" (Exodus 32:5 KJV). Singing songs about God, professing to dance before God, naming the name of God is proof of and testimony to nothing. It should also be remembered that such all take place under the banner of "church," a "feast to the LORD" (Exodus 32:5 KJV) in the "Temple": the very same scene of Ezekiel's bad dream. There is a line and a limit we need to recognise, remember, and return to: "for thou hast magnified thy word above all thy name" (Psalm 138:2 KJV).

This sleeping giant the church has become, so much like Samson, can also – and *must* also – learn from Samson, who in his needless blindness discovered that "the hair on his head began to grow again" (Judges 16:22 KJV) and "saw" enough again to pray: "O Lord GOD, remember me, I pray thee, and strengthen me, I pray thee, only this once" (Judges 16:28 KJV).

God did it again for Samson, and He will do it again for us, His church. I don't want to miss Him and what He will do, even just one more time. However, before we realise any *construction,* we will have to realise some *destruction.*

2

Declaration

"LORD, thou hast been favourable unto thy land: thou hast brought back the captivity of Jacob. Thou hast forgiven the iniquity of thy people, thou hast covered all their sin. Selah. Thou hast taken away all thy wrath: thou hast turned thyself from the fierceness of thine anger."
(Psalm 85:1–3 KJV)

"Selah: Consider These Things!"

Psalm 85 bears the title *"For the director of music. Of the Sons of Korah. A Psalm"* (KJV). The Levitical Temple Choir was appointed by King David to serve in the worship of God (see 1 Chronicles 9). What is worship but declaration?

Beginning with the Psalms and continuing into the New Testament, the scriptural, historical, traditional songs and hymns of the church primarily tell the story of God. For example, in the time of the

Wesleys, where many could not read, the lyrics of hymns and songs became great teaching tools for communicating the truths of the Faith. The lyrics of such frequently contained words and phrases lifted straight from the Bible. Nowadays, a major shift has taken place in this regard. From being centred around "the God I experience," much of modern music – and thus worship – is preoccupied with "my experience of God." Where Scripture used to mark the boundaries and set the pace, "my experience" is now the guide, guardian, and glory. "The Story of God" in large part plays second fiddle to "The Story of Self." This is furthered by the style of much modern worship music. The steady rhythm of the more traditional hymn of yesterday, along with the melody, is well suited for a congregation of any number to enter in to and enjoy. Whereas the irregular tempo of many modern worship songs, in unpredictable melodies, not to mention the mindlessly even moronically repetitive lyrics, become exclusive of congregational participation in favour of the performance of the prominent and presumed elect at the front. Worship ministers, in conjunction with the musicians, are meant to lead, enable, and accompany the congregation, not render them obsolete, by outdoing the worshippers and upstaging God. Worship composers and leaders should pay close attention to the likes of Psalm 85, where the story – and the glory – is God's.

God Can Do It Again

After attending church one Sunday and before getting into bed, a little boy knelt to say his prayers: "God, what a great time we had in church today. You should have been there!"

This is the declaration of the opening verses of Psalm 85: "God, you should have been there! We need you to be in our midst today like you were with those who came before us.... God can do it again!"

The Occasion

Many suggest that the occasion being referred to in these first verses of Psalm 85 was the return from exile, even pointing back and linking us to Ezekiel's days of exile. Being in exile is to be where you don't belong and how you never intended to be. Ronald F. Youngblood describes Psalm 85 as "a communal prayer for the renewal of God's mercies to His people at a time when they are *once more* [emphasis mine] suffering distress".[4] We have been here before – in the exile of disobedience and distress – which must also mean we can repent and return, being restored and revived again.

Is the church today not also in a place of exile: being where we don't belong and how we should never be, because it was never intended and doesn't need to be? God not being in our midst as He desires and we need Him to be, with many no longer believing He can: this is surely to be in exile.

Leonard Ravenhill captured the snapshot of our plight today as the people of God when he pointedly observed, "Let 20% of the Church choir fail to turn up for practice and the choir leader is deflated. Let 20% of the Church members turn up for the Prayer Meeting and the Pastor is elated!"[5] Something, somewhere is seriously wrong, sadly absent, and tragically out of place … exiled.

The Location

When you think of revival, what is it you imagine and see and expect? Oftentimes, if a church service runs over its usual time, people foolishly talk of revival, or they picture revival as crowds of people flocking to and packing the local church and getting saved. However, revival is *not* evangelism. Paul Rees helps us to understand: "Revival and evangelism, although closely related, are not to be [confused]. Revival is an experience of the Church – evangelism is the expression of the Church."[6]

Indeed, the Bible itself bears this out in what it understands of the condition of Salvation. In Ephesians 2:1, the un-saved are "dead in trespasses and sins" (KJV). How can you therefore "revive" what is "dead" because it has never been alive? You can only revive what has been alive, and the un-saved have never been alive to God. The Bible goes on to tell us in Ephesians 2:5 that in salvation, we are "made alive" (NIV). It is those who are "alive" who need to be revived. The most alive Christ-Ones are the newest, often putting the older ones to shame because they just believe God. Surely the most vibrant, effective Christ-Ones should be those who have known and trusted and walked with God the longest and deepest and farthest, but yet often ….

Have you ever considered that the church needs reviving, including self, beginning with self?

When he pastored in Leeds, England, Samuel Chadwick once visited a lady whose husband had died. They had been arranging the funeral service when the bereaved wife asked Chadwick for a favour. She said, "My husband is unshaven and I would like him to be buried clean-shaven. Please would you ask the barber to come and shave him?" Chadwick did so. It was night when the barber got there, and the only light he had was a candle. The deceased was quite a big man, and the barber could not reach across him. The widow was downstairs, and so he placed the candle on the man's chest and climbed on top. As the weight of his body pressed down on the dead man, the corpse sat up and blew out the candle! The barber ran screaming from the house. The body still had air – but no breath of life. Is that not our condition today? We can still get responses from the body. Press certain places, and we still get air – a lot of it hot air – but it's the embers of the members who were alive yesterday, no longer today. We need reviving.

Such is the location of the declaration: "thy land ... Jacob ... thy people." Us ... you ... me.

The Authentication

Many were badly burned and seriously let down by the false revival dawns of Toronto and Pensacola, and others will be again when the bubble of the Emerging Church and the New Apostolic Reformation finally bursts, proving to be another cluster of promising but disappointing "clouds ... without rain" (Jude 12 KJV). Such is not a reason for smug congratulation of us who perceive these things; we may never get burned here. Our danger is that in questioning everything, we find ourselves at the equally wrong and other extreme of believing and expecting and experiencing nothing.

We must maintain the trusted ground and wise balance of Scripture: "Quench not the Spirit. Despise not prophesyings. Prove all things; hold fast that which is good. Abstain from all appearance of evil" (1 Thessalonians 5:19–22 KJV). We must understand that just because something is proclaimed as being "from God" and testified to as "of God" does not make it so. In our hunger and desperation for God to move in revival, we must learn the lessons of our recent past, see the dangers of the present predicament, and not grab at the first suggestions without authenticating the signs. It is important that we not only look for and listen to what is being said and done but also to what is not.

Will God really come to where and among whom He is neither feared or revered? He is God Almighty, *not* God-All-Matey. When God truly shows up, the first thing that happens is not dancing but dread. Reverence is lacking in the church of today. We have bowed to the relaxed, laid-back culture that resents authority, rubbishes decency, and resists order, not to mention dignity. We have been deceived by the enemy of our souls that to win the world, we must become like the very world people need to be saved and delivered from. This world is being entertained all the way to hell, and the church is part of the programme.

To "authenticate" is to show and prove genuineness, truth, validity. This is done by testing what is claimed by the measure and marks of what distinguishes and identifies it from the artificial, the false, and the flawed.

It was A.W. Tozer who drew the contrast between the "new cross that entertains and the old cross that slew."[7] Pastor Gary Gilley does a fine job in drawing together some key observations we do well to keep in focus over what is being promoted and accepted today at the expense of what has been departed from in our yesterday:

- The old gospel is about an offended God. The new gospel is about a wounded self.
- The old gospel is about sin. The new gospel is about needs.
- The old gospel is about our need for forgiveness. The new gospel is about our need for fulfilment.
- The old gospel is offensive to those who are perishing. The new gospel is attractive and amusing and affirming.[8]

God Is the Source and Controller of Revival

We see this in who is emphasised in the declaration of Psalm 85. The most we can do is "get ready" for revival – it is not a formula, nor is it manufactured or scheduled in on the church diary. Wilbur Smith contended, "Revival is from God or it is no revival at all."[9] Revival may be our invitation, but it is always God's initiative, His intrusion, invasion, and interruption, even incision.

Specifically, here is where the incision comes:

A) Sin Is Never Ignored but Always Removed in Revival

How can we expect to draw closer to God and yet have sin remain unchallenged, overlooked, and unconfessed? Tozer contended, "It is useless for large companies of believers to spend long hours begging God to send Revival. Unless we intend to reform we may as well not pray."[10] Leonard Ravenhill noted how we "appease" sin where we should be "opposing" it. Toronto and Pensacola, along with Emerging Church and New Apostolic Reformation, are marred by hilarity and brashness over self, not marked by humility and brokenness over sin, in the awareness that we have grieved God. Perhaps the greatest sign of the decline of the church is not to be measured numerically but in terms of morality. The church is so like the world in what we accept, affirm, applaud, and allow. The cost of being so wide in what we have embraced is shallowness in what we believe and how we behave.

The truth is: the closer we get to God, the deeper we go with Him, the more our sense personal sin increases, not in condemnation, but in our need for cleansing. People talk about being saved and forgiven – but is that enough? Specifically, what have we been saved from and forgiven for?

- a sharp tongue that runs away with us?
- a foul mouth that poisons the atmosphere we occupy?
- an appetite so out of control that it becomes an unhealthy and ugly addiction?
- a lust-filled mind which horrifies us in our more honest and better moments?
- a short temper which causes hurt to others and much regret to ourselves?

Charles Finney opened his classic work on revival with these words:

Self-examination consists in looking at your lives, in considering your actions, in calling up the past, and learning its true character. Look back over your past history. Take up your individual sins one by one, and look at them. I do not mean that you should just cast a glance at your past life, and see that it has been full of sins, and then go to God and make a sort of general confession, and ask for pardon. That is not the way. You must take them up one by one. It will be a good thing to take a pen and paper, as you go over them, and write them down as they occur to you. Go over them as carefully as a merchant goes over his books; and as often as a sin comes before your memory, add it to the list. General confessions of sin will never do. Your sins were committed one by one; and as far as you can come at them, they ought to be reviewed and repented of one by one.[11]

B) In Revival, the Preoccupation Is with God and Being Made Right with Him

In revival, there is such a holy awareness of God, without a note being played, a song being sung, even a sermon preached, or an altar invitation extended. Oh, for the day when the one thing people will not be able to do when they come to our churches is nothing – they will either stay and get right with God or get out. Isaiah said, "The sinners in Zion are afraid; fearfulness hath surprised the hypocrites" (Isaiah 33:14 KJV). How true: no revival ever fed the ego of man or encouraged superficiality; there is no time and no place for that. Scripture and history teach us that when revival comes, the clock goes out the window; the church hardly closes, schedules are suspended because eternity is in view, and lives are transformed, not just for a moment, but in a moment for good.

When revival comes, today's "feel-good, go to church once a week, give a token offering, sing your happy songs, and all in sixty minutes" Christianity many have settled for and promoted, with even more having never known any other way, will be seen for what it is: farcical and false, at best an "escaping through the flames" (1 Corinthians 3:15, NIV), if even that be so.

In his book, *Losing Our Virtue: Why the Church Must Recover Its Moral Vision,* David F. Wells is on target when he writes:

> Can the church view people as consumers without inevitably forgetting that they are sinners? Can the church promote the gospel as a product and not forget that those who buy it must repent? Can the church market itself and not forget that it does not belong to itself but to Christ? Can the church pursue success in the market place and not lose its Biblical faithfulness?[12]

In ditching the definition and thus distinction of what it truly means to be saved and lost, whereby we treat the lost sinner as if he were not, we have dishonoured God and visited a great disservice upon the gospel and the souls of humanity.

Let me close this chapter with three quotes for further reflection:

> I wonder if we often expect too little? Do we think negatively more often than not? I think that many times we have a crushing sense of how improbable our dreams and desires for the Church are, and then push them to the back of our minds and settle – settle for mediocrity and dullness, if not lethargy and apathy. I don't want to be someone who settles.[13]

Do not we rest in our day too much on the arm of flesh? Cannot the same wonders be done now as of old? Do not the eyes of the Lord still run to and fro throughout the whole earth to show Himself strong on behalf of those who put their trust in Him? Oh, that God would give me more practical faith in Him! Where is now the Lord God of Elijah? He is waiting for Elijah to call on Him.[14]

O Breath of life, come sweeping through us,
Revive Your church with life and power.
O Breath of life, come, cleanse, renew us,
And fit Your church to meet this hour.

O Wind of God, come bend us, break us,
Till humbly we confess our need;
Then in Your tenderness remake us,
Revive, restore, for this we plead.

O Breath of love, come breathe within us,
Renewing thought and will and heart;
Come, Love of Christ, afresh to win us,
Revive Your church in every part.

Revive us, Lord! Is zeal abating
while harvest fields are vast and white?
Revive us, Lord, the world is waiting,
Equip Your church to spread the light.[15]

3

Desperation

*"Turn us, O God of our salvation, and cause
thine anger toward us to cease.
Wilt thou be angry with us for ever? wilt thou draw
out thine anger to all generations? Wilt thou not revive
us again: that thy people may rejoice in thee?
Shew us thy mercy, O LORD, and grant us thy salvation."*
(Psalm 85:4–7 KJV)

A pastor was bemoaning the condition of the congregation to a board member; he said, "What do you think the problem is? Ignorance or apathy?" The church officer replied, "I don't know and I don't care." Many don't ….

There is only one group of people who ever get revival:

- Not the Diligent, who work hard and are so organised and have no place to "fit" revival.

- Not the Devoted, those who are walking in God's holiness because they don't need reviving.
- Not the Distracted, who are concerned and bound up with Martha's "many things" at the expense of any time, energy, or inclination for Mary's "good [thing]" (see Luke 10:38– 42 KJV).
- Neither is it the Distant, who are so out of touch with God, stalling and stopping at His hand, not striving and seeking after His heart.
- It is the Desperate who get revival: those who "know" and "care."

How easy it is to talk and sing, and even read, about revival.

In Luke 6:12, the Bible tells us that when it came to choosing His twelve Disciples, Jesus – the Son of God – first spent the whole night before in prayer. Can you imagine the changes to local church and denominational leadership there would be if those involved in the choosing process, either by election or appointment, were to first and before spend the night praying? Jesus also informs us that there are some things which "come ... but by prayer and fasting" (Mark 9:29 KJV). Are grave matters such as these not in that category?

In increasing measure, the longer it has been my privilege to be a pastor, when it comes to recommending leaders, my first port of call is not with those who are found in the pulpit or some other prominent position of responsibility. I have learned – mostly through error – to begin and end with those who are in regular, committed, participatory attendance at the prayer meetings of the local church. It was Leonard Ravenhill who keenly observed that today's church elects and appoints men of "standing" in their reputations and no longer men of "kneeling" in a proven testimony of righteous living (see 1 Timothy 3 and 5). For too long, we have appointed and elected leaders in the unconfirmed hope they will be approved and not because they have first been approved and tested according to the measure of Scripture.

Significantly, the Bible does not record one instance of the Disciples asking Jesus, "Teach us to preach... Teach us to sing... Teach us to discuss and debate... Teach us to take notes... Teach us to know what resources to buy ... Teach us how to promote causes and organise conferences."

The Bible tells us that it was after witnessing Jesus praying that they said, "Lord, teach us to pray" (Luke 11:1 KJV). What right do we have to condemn the removal of prayer from our schools and other public forums when we have largely removed prayer from our own local churches? Is there not something drastically wrong in that many will have church and do church on Sunday, whether God is there or not? Even more tragic is to not even know the difference. The Holy Spirit was given and the church birthed in a prayer meeting, not a preaching meeting.

Often when a local church discovers that there is a vacationing pastor among the congregation, he is identified and invited to bring a few words of greeting. On one occasion, a visiting pastor, having been given the opportunity, said this: "You can tell how popular a Church is by who comes on Sunday morning. You can tell how popular the pastor is by who comes on Sunday night. You can tell how popular Jesus is by who comes to the Prayer Meeting".[16]

In following Christ, who prayed all night, in the awareness of the need to fast in the face of certain things, in the light of the Disciples' request "teach us to pray," how can we continue in our other ways, holding on to our lesser things?

- Praying for revival is more than expressing the sentiment of wishful thinking.

- Praying for revival is more than a quick sentence and takes more than five minutes, now and then.
- Praying for revival is more than just talking about it.
- Praying for revival will crucify our pride.
- Praying for revival will break our hearts.
- Praying for revival will steal our time.
- Praying for revival will keep us awake at night.
- Praying for revival is never easy or convenient.
- Praying for revival is not popular and never applauded.
- Praying for revival can never be only in public.
- Praying for revival keeps praying until God answers.
- Praying for revival is more than just an afterthought when we have been reminded because another has prompted us.
- Praying for revival never leaves us the same.

The Confession of Desperation

There are two words in Psalm 85:4–7 in regard to God which we rarely hear coming from pulpits today: "wrath" and "anger" (KJV). Such suggestions are alien, having been dropped from the vocabulary of the modern church in favour of the "Seeker Sensitive" mantra: "Thus saith the Lord, 'I have nothing against you … as far as I know!" The so-called experts from the church growth movement tell us, "Don't rock the boat. Always send people away affirmed and confirmed – happy. We don't want to lose people by scaring them away. We need to give them what they have come for." The enemy of our souls has whispered to many a faithful pastor, "The people are tired. Give them something light and fluffy. They are burdened. Give them something nice and easy and shallow. Skim, pamper, tickle, amuse – don't probe and press or question and challenge."

When such are the method and the message, there is nothing to be desperate over because there is nothing to confess. A person who is protected – because he has never been led and allowed – from getting to the place of being keenly aware of the gravity of his own sinful condition before a holy God will never come to repentance and come through in salvation. This is what we have departed from and been distracted from in large part in the so-called gospel presentations of what passes as preaching today.

Is this not what we find in much of today's church? Little hunger for God; for better or for worse, appetite is an accurate indicator of health. Obsessively preoccupied with the clock lest the sermon runs over twenty minutes and the service lasts more than an hour – yet no urgency over eternity. No burden of concern over the fate of lost souls, the condition of the backslider, and the Peter Pan Christian who never grows up. The cross of Christ may still stir the emotions for the duration of an emotive song but does not move us to the depths of genuine awe and surrender in personal transformation that gets beyond the church car park and into the home and the workplace on Monday because it's truly "in" the heart, not just "by" heart. Keith Green catches many with his potent lyric: "Jesus rose from the dead – but you can't even get out of bed."[17]

This generation is not the first to be like it is. The Revelation of Jesus Christ records letters He addressed to seven local churches. He writes to Laodicea (Revelation 3:14–22 KJV):

> These things saith the Amen, the faithful and true witness, the beginning of the creation of God; I know thy works, that thou art neither cold nor hot: I would thou wert cold or hot. So then because thou art lukewarm, and neither cold nor hot, I will spue thee out of my mouth. Because thou sayest, I am rich, and increased with goods, and have need of nothing; and knowest not that thou

art wretched, and miserable, and poor, and blind, and naked.

Revival never comes to the self-satisfied.

> I counsel thee to buy of me gold tried in the fire, that thou mayest be rich; and white raiment, that thou mayest be clothed, and that the shame of thy nakedness do not appear; and anoint thine eyes with eyesalve, that thou mayest see.

"Laodicea" is derived from the two Greek words for *"people"* and *"rule"*: The church where the people rule. No wonder they (and we) got themselves into such a mess.

> As many as I love, I rebuke and chasten: be zealous therefore, and repent. Behold, I stand at the door, and knock: if any man hear my voice, and open the door, I will come in to him, and will sup with him, and he with me. To him that overcometh will I grant to sit with me in my throne, even as I also overcame, and am set down with my Father in his throne!

This is not an appeal to the unregenerate world, but the redeemed church.

"He that hath an ear, let him hear what the Spirit saith unto the churches."

We don't have endless time to further wait and wander. Now is the time.

There are two elements always present in desperation:

A) **Honesty** – no more fudging and excusing and justifying self: "God, you have a reason to be angry because of who we are and what we do."

B) **Humility** – no more serving and preserving and comparing and congratulating self: "Whatever it takes, God, revive us! You have a right to be angry because of who You are."

The Cry of Desperation

There are many who say they are desperate – for "that" and over "this" – but yet they are still in control, calling the shots, making the decisions, setting the pace. True desperation neither affords these luxuries nor takes such liberties.

In Psalm 85, the Psalmist cries, "Wilt thou not revive us again: that thy people may rejoice in thee? [God, revival is our only hope and revival comes from none but You]" (KJV). Elsewhere, another Psalm cries, "Rivers of waters run down mine eyes, because they keep not thy law" (Psalm 119:136 KJV). Jeremiah cried, "Oh that my head were waters, and mine eyes a fountain of tears, that I might weep day and night for the slain of the daughter of my people!" (Jeremiah 9:1 KJV). The apostle Paul cried, "I could wish that myself were accursed from Christ for my brethren, my kinsmen according to the flesh" (Romans 9:3 KJV). Then there was Rachel in Genesis 30:1: "Give me children, or else I die" (KJV).

Rachel was beautiful but barren, as are many churches and individual Christ-Ones. Evidencing little spiritual fruit, bearing no spiritual children, seeing only ourselves as marking the natural end of the life of the local church, because there is no supernatural life beyond us in those we have led to Christ and nurtured in the Faith to continue the work. Surely, we don't have the luxury nor can we take the liberty of further ignoring, maintaining, and justifying the barrenness we have for too long allowed ourselves to become accustomed to, blaming the culture or whatever else, when, in the words of Shakespeare's Cassius, "The fault, dear Brutus, is not in our stars / But in ourselves".[18] In the church, we talk of shepherds and sheep, but shepherds don't give birth to sheep; sheep give birth to sheep. We have put the onus of expectation and responsibility for productivity on the pastor who is the shepherd, while the sheep in the pews just sit back, arms folded, waiting to be amused, impressed, and entertained, leaving the church service no better off than if they had just left a sports game or a night at the theatre. The pastor is among the ones who are to help equip and enable the people, as the shepherd does the sheep (see Ephesians 4:11–15), but there are some things only sheep can and should do.

Leonard Ravenhill pursued this same line of "beautiful but barren" when he wrote,

> "Oh, the reproach of our barren altars! Has the Holy Ghost delight in our electric organs, carpeted aisles, and new decorations" (nowadays, it would be slick PowerPoints, flashing lights, and loud music) "if the crib is empty? Never! Oh that the deathlike stillness of the sanctuary could be shattered by the blessed cry of newborn babes! … Shamed at the impotence of the Church, chagrined at the monopoly the devil holds, shall we not cry with tortured spirits (and mean it): 'Give me children, or else I die!'"[19]

The Cost of Desperation

It was General Dwight Eisenhower who said, "There are no victories at discount prices."[20] So it is with revival; revival always costs because it never leaves us the same.

A local church was cited by the police for being a "general nuisance." The crime was playing the hymn "Now Thank We All Our God,"[21] on the church chimes. When requested by the City Council to come to some accommodation, the pastor agreed to turn down the volume and shorten the period of hymn playing from eighteen to five minutes a day. The pastor explained, "We don't want to be a nuisance." Is this not our problem? We want to follow Christ without cost, with no upheaval or inconvenience, incurring no wrath from anyone. As Pastor Randall Denney put it, "We want to serve Christ in a way that doesn't offend the devil."[22] On this point alone, the question needs to be asked as to how seriously the church today takes belief in the enemy of our souls at all? For some, that is a devastating indictment and the cause of defeat, beginning in the home.

There is much to be learned from an incident the New Testament book of Acts records for us:

> And [Paul] went into the synagogue, and spake boldly for the space of three months, disputing and persuading the things concerning the kingdom of God. But when divers were hardened, and believed not, but spake evil of that way before the multitude, he departed from them, and separated the disciples, disputing daily in the school of one Tyrannus. And this continued by the space of two years; so that all they which dwelt in Asia heard the word of the Lord Jesus, both Jews and Greeks. And God wrought special miracles by the hands of Paul: So that from his body were brought unto the sick handkerchiefs or aprons, and the diseases departed from them, and the evil spirits went out of them. Then certain of the vagabond Jews, exorcists, took upon them to call over them which had evil spirits the name of the Lord Jesus, saying, We adjure you by Jesus

whom Paul preacheth. And there were seven sons
of one Sceva, a Jew, and chief of the priests, which
did so. And the evil spirit answered and said, Jesus
I know, and Paul I know; but who are ye? And the
man in whom the evil spirit was leaped on them,
and overcame them, and prevailed against them, so
that they fled out of that house naked and wounded
(Acts 19:8–16 KJV).

Not only will revival impact all our relationships, interfere with our
plans, and revolutionise our outlook, it will also make us nuisances
to the devil, and we will become known in hell. The price of that is
always a cross, never a cushion. Unlike the cushion, the cross is not
a place of sleeping but of sacrifice.

God answered Rachel's prayer for children. She died in giving birth
to Benjamin (see Genesis 35:18). "Give me children, or else I die" was
not just a plea but became a price. Jacob also knew about a price. At
the place he would later call "Peniel" in wrestling for the blessing of
God, he got it but was permanently marked, even injured, because
of it, never to leave him the same (see Genesis 32:22–32). Even the
Christ of God Himself discovered this: "who for the joy that was set
before him endured the cross, despising the shame, and is set down
at the right hand of the throne of God" (Hebrews 12:2 KJV). There
are no victories at discount prices.

Many years ago, the Christian magazine *Conquest for Christ* included
these words from a church leader in India:

The indigenous churches in India have a great
burden for [the West] and are praying that God
will visit [you] with revival. You feel sorry for us
in India because of our poverty in material things.
We who know the Lord in India feel sorry for you

in [the West] because of your spiritual poverty. We pray that God may give you "gold tried in the fire" (Revelation 3:17, 18 KJV), which He has promised to those who know the power of His resurrection.... In our churches we spend four or five or six hours in prayer and worship, and frequently our people wait on the Lord in prayer all night; but in [the West], after you have been in church for one hour, you begin to look at your watch. We pray that God may open your eyes to the true meaning of worship. To attract people to meetings, you have a great dependence on posters, on advertising, on promotion, and on the build-up of a human being; in India, we have nothing more than the Lord Himself, and we find that He is sufficient. Before a Christian meeting in India we never announce who the speaker will be. When the people come, they come to seek the Lord and not a human being or to hear some special favourite speaking to them. We have had as many as 12,000 people come together just to worship the Lord and to have fellowship together. We are praying that the people in [the West] might also come to church with a hunger for God and not merely a hunger to see some form of amusement or hear choirs or the voice of any man.[23]

There is much for us to urgently contemplate here, to courageously contend for and honestly and humbly confront over. These words from Jonathan Goforth help to push us even further in the needful and right direction of desperation:

Our reading of the Word of God makes it inconceivable to us that the Holy Spirit should be willing, even for a day, to delay His work. We may be sure that, where there is a lack of the fullness of God, it is ever due to man's lack of faith and obedience. If God the Holy Spirit is not glorifying Jesus Christ in the world today, as at Pentecost, it is we who are to blame. After all, what is revival but simply the Spirit of God fully controlling in the surrendered life? It must always be possible, then, when man yields. The sin of unyieldedness, alone, can keep us from revival.

But are we ready to receive Him? Do we value the Giver and the gift sufficiently? Are we ready to pay the price of Holy Ghost revival? Take prayer for example. The history of revival shows plainly that all movements of the Spirit have started in prayer. Yet is it not right there that many of us wilt and falter at the cost?

"What is the secret of revival?" a great evangelist was once asked. "There is no secret," he replied. "Revival always comes in answer to prayer."[24]

4

Separation

"I will hear what God the LORD will speak: for
he will speak peace unto his people, and to his
saints: but let them not turn again to folly. Surely
his salvation is nigh them that fear him; that
glory may dwell in our land.

Mercy and truth are met together; righteousness
and peace have kissed each other.

Truth shall spring out of the earth; and
righteousness shall look down from heaven.

Yea, the LORD shall give that which is good; and
our land shall yield her increase.

Righteousness shall go before him; and shall set
us in the way of his steps."

(Psalm 85:8–13 KJV)

Dialogues of the Deaf

In his book, *To Understand Each Other,* Dr. Paul Tournier observed, "Listen to the conversations of our world, between nations as well as couples. They are for the most part dialogues of the deaf".[25] Nations talk over nations, spouses talk at each other, and the number one complaint from teenagers about parents is exactly the top accusation parents express regarding their teenaged children: "They don't listen."

Once there was a man who dared God to speak: "Burn the bush like You did for Moses, God, and I will follow! ... Collapse the walls like You did for Joshua, God, and I will fight! ... Still the waves like You did on Galilee, God, and I will listen!" So the man sat by a bush, near a wall, close to the sea, and waited for God to speak.

God heard the man and answered:

- He sent fire, not for a bush, but for a church.
- He brought down a wall, not of brick, but of sin.
- He stilled a storm, not of the sea, but of a soul.

Then God waited for the man to respond ... and waited ... and waited ... and waited. But because the man was looking at bushes, not hearts, ... bricks, not lives, ... seas, not souls, he decided that God had done nothing.

Finally, he looked to God and asked, "God, have You lost Your power?"

God looked at the man and said, "Man, have you lost your hearing?"[26]

I Will Listen to What God the Lord Will Say

Everything that is of the world is set against us hearing God – and so, many of us don't. We are bombarded with noise. From the minute we wake up in the morning to the moment our heads hit the pillow at night, noise: the radio, television, we now carry it all with us on those smart phones, which do not serve to make us very ... smart. So conditioned to and confined by noise has this generation become that young people are now requesting to be allowed to listen to music via headphones even as they sit their school exams, arguing that they cannot function without noise. Social media is inherently antisocial because of what it sacrifices: real face time in favour of artificial FaceTime. The immediateness of these means of communications – constantly back and forth, trying to better the previous comment – has resulted in many foolish words, shamed faces, ruined relationships, and damaged testimonies, all because of a lack of time and space to think.

We are also overwhelmed by activity, even to the extent that our recreation exhausts us. The church is not immune to any of this. We have little time for stillness, and in worship, there seems to be an unspoken fear of silence, as we seek to fill every minute with activity and every moment with noise, no matter how senseless and unsound it may be.

Separation is the key.

The Position of Separation

By implication, this involves conscious intention. It comes neither naturally nor easily; it must be decided, cultivated, nurtured, and protected. So long as silence is an absentee in our lives and stillness the sacrificed casualty of our schedules, getting into the position of separation is just not going to happen. The fast lane is for passing, not meeting.

Again and again, the gospel accounts of Jesus tell us that He went off by Himself to pray. Why? "I will hear what God the LORD will speak." The Bible also records for us Jesus, in healing a person, taking him aside – away from the atmosphere of unbelief. Jesus also sought to bring His disciples away from the rush of demands and the pressure of people (see Mark 7:33 and 6:31).

Consider these two Scripture verses side by side:

"Be still, and know that I am God" (Psalm 46:10 KJV).

"And [Jesus] arose, and rebuked the wind, and said unto the sea, Peace, be still" (Mark 4:39 KJV).

Who is being addressed in Psalm 46:10? The very same as in Mark 4:39.

"Be Still, My Soul"[27] is a great hymn, the favourite of many – including myself – having brought comfort to countless souls. However, "my soul" is not the original application of this command to "Be still, and know that I am God." Verse 10 continues, "I will be exalted in the HEATHEN" (KJV); verse 6 tells us, "The HEATHEN raged" (KJV). Verse 10 concludes, "I will be exalted in the EARTH" (KJV). Verses 1–2 of Psalm 46 speak of the "earth [being] removed" (KJV). We already know what God says to the wind and waves in Mark 4:39: "Be still!" Literally, "Enough! ... Leave off!" We have to come to the place where we let God deal with and speak to the elements of our chaotic worlds, which bombard and drown us, that we might hear God, getting into that needful and right place with Him, that we too will know what it is to "Be still, and know that [He] is God." Before God speaks that to us, we need to first allow Him to speak it to that which troubles and takes from us. That means seeking God to deliberately come aside with Him – coming apart that we might not come apart.

> Therefore also now, saith the LORD, turn ye even
> to me with all your heart, and with fasting, and with
> weeping, and with mourning: And rend your heart,

and not your garments, and turn unto the LORD your God: for he is gracious and merciful, slow to anger, and of great kindness, and repenteth him of the evil. Who knoweth if he will return and repent, and leave a blessing behind him; even a meat offering and a drink offering unto the LORD your God?

Blow the trumpet in Zion, sanctify a fast, call a solemn assembly: Gather the people, sanctify the congregation, assemble the elders, gather the children, and those that suck the breasts: let the bridegroom go forth of his chamber, and the bride out of her closet. Let the priests, the ministers of the LORD, weep between the porch and the altar, and let them say, Spare thy people, O LORD, and give not thine heritage to reproach, that the heathen should rule over them: wherefore should they say among the people, Where is their God?

(Joel 2:12–17 KJV)

What is the message here but, "Separation! Find the place and get into the position of hearing God. Stop what you are doing." I know that many who read this will say, "Don't you realise how busy I am? The responsibilities I have?" Notice who God calls to the place of separation: "Gather the people, sanctify the congregation, assemble the elders, gather the children, and those that suck the breasts: let the bridegroom go forth of his chamber, and the bride out of her closet" (KJV). Does it ever get more pressing and important than these?

Most are more familiar with the verse of promised revival that comes later in Joel 2:25: "I will restore to you the years that the locust hath eaten" (KJV). Before we see the restoration condition of Joel 2:25, we have to know and be found in the separation position of Joel 2:12–17.

In a former place of pastoral ministry, the local churches got together and produced an information leaflet for the community. My heart was broken, for between all the churches and their listed programmes and activities and services, there was only one prayer meeting. Leonard Ravenhill wrote of the very same plight:

> "Rent hearts are not found easily amongst us these days. To most of us, fasting is out, tears are frowned upon, and mourning is associated with melancholia. How wise we are! But you will notice (and maybe notice it with pain) we have no revival. We are wondering why God does not move; He is wondering why we do not break! We have His exceeding great and precious promises and wonder why He does not oblige; He wonders why we do not obey! We wish He would bend low; He wishes we would break down".[28]

The Promise of Separation

A) **Peace:** Jesus is the "Prince of Peace" (Isaiah 9:6 KJV), and yet many of His own have no peace. Nervous about this, agitated over that, terrified of nearly everything. When the peace goes – or has never been there – so the joy goes (or never gets there). "The joy of the LORD is your strength" (Nehemiah 8:10 KJV). Don't we think the enemy of our souls knows that and works to keep us from being in the position where we can see and hear and know it? "They that wait upon the LORD shall renew their strength; they shall mount up with wings as eagles; they shall run, and not be weary; and they shall walk, and not faint" (Isaiah 40:31 KJV). Some are anything and any way but that.

I know there are those who will see this as insensitive and not trying to understand, but I base my words, not on the psychology of our day, or the popular "theology" from our modern pulpits, which pampers and excuses, even when to do so is detrimental and just plain wrong. My contention regarding the state of many Christ-Ones in their minds, emotions and bodies is based squarely on God's promise of our separation to Him: "for he will speak peace unto his people" (KJV).

"I am the Vine; ye are the branches.... Abide in Me.... Abide in My Words.... Abide in My Love.... Abide in My joy.... Abide in My promises" (John 15:5ff KJV). We do well to meditate on these words of Jesus considering what/who we are separated from ... that we might be separated to.

B) Protection

> A Christian is a man who feels
> repentance on a Sunday
> for what he did on Saturday
> and is going to do on Monday![29]

Have we not followed and settled in that miserable cycle for long enough? "But let them not turn again to folly" (KJV). This warning is also an implicit promise. How can you "turn again to folly" from this position of separation to God? You cannot return if you "remain." It's when we forsake this place of separation that we "turn again" to what and where and how we were. It is when God no longer fills us from the centre, and we try to reduce Him to fit our overcrowded lives that having been rightly turned, we "turn [wrong] again." When we forget God we are bound – literally – to turn again to folly.

Charles Finney wrote:

> The unbelief of the Church as to what they may
> receive from Christ, is the great stumbling-block,

hindering themselves and others from experiencing deliverance. Not only is this a great curse to professed Christians, but it is also a great grief to Jesus Christ and a sore trial.

Many seem to have hardened their hearts against all expectation of this deliverance from sin. They have heard the doctrine preached. They have seen some profess to be in this state of salvation from sin, but they have also seen some of this class fall again, and now they deliberately reject the whole doctrine. But is this consistent with really embracing the gospel? What is Christ to the believer? What was His errand into the world? What is He doing and what is He trying to do?

He has come to break the power of sin in the heart, and to be the life of the believer, working in him a perpetual salvation from sin, aiming to bring him thus, and only thus, to Heaven at last. What is faith, what but the actual giving of yourself up to Christ that He may do this work for you and in you! What are you to believe of Christ if not this, that He is to save His people from their sins? Can you tell of anything else? Does the Bible tell you to expect something different and less than this? The fact is, that it has been the great stumbling-block to the Church that this thing has not been well understood. The common experience of nominal Christians has misrepresented and belied the truth. The masses forming their views much more from this experience than from the Bible, or at best applying this experience to interpret the Bible, have adopted exceedingly defective, not to say false, opinions as to the nature and design of the Gospel.[30]

C) Presence

An African "Mother in Israel" said, "You white folks meet to prove the existence of God; we black folks meet to experience the presence of God." Very astute.

How is our sense of the sacred, not just for the duration of a Sunday service, but in all our lives? If we were as consciously convinced of the nearness of God as the songs we sing say we are, we would not be how we are. We need to remind ourselves that it is just as much a sin to *sing* a lie than to *preach* a lie! A.W. Tozer candidly observed, "The Christian conception of God … is so decadent as to be utterly beneath the dignity of the Most High God and actually to constitute for professed believers something amounting to a moral calamity".[31] In the same book, Tozer also states, "With our loss of the sense of majesty has come the further loss of religious awe and consciousness of the divine Presence. We have lost our spirit of worship and our ability to withdraw inwardly to meet God in adoring silence".[32] Jacob's claim, "Surely the LORD is in this place, and I knew it not" (Genesis 28:16 KJV), was not an excuse but a confession.

The Purpose of Separation

Pure and simply, the "glory" of God is the purpose of separation. Revival is for our benefit but always, only, ever, for God's glory. Revival does not make us look good; it glorifies God. Revival will never promote the knowledge of a church (denomination), but it will spread the knowledge of Christ. Revival makes us holy, not heroes, Again, this is specifically where and why Toronto and Pensacola, along with Emerging Church and New Apostolic Reformation, fail(ed) the test. David Wilkerson succinctly closes the argument: "You cannot import a revival!"[33]

It is important for us that we do not miss the inclusion of the word "fear" in Psalm 85:9. This is another truth-factor that is dangerously missing amongst the people of God today. John Burton has written an excellent article titled, "Is It Time for Hell Fire Preaching Again?"[34] (*Charisma News*, July 2015). He writes, "God is much more interested in the establishment of His name and His Word than He is in the feelings or desires of individuals, or even of entire regions. This is God's nature." When we understand that the basic meaning of the Hebrew word "glory" is "weightiness, heaviness," we begin to appreciate the need of, connection with, and place for reverent "fear."

Burton continues,

> "We have mistaken God as One Who is always happy and passive, like that sweet grandfather who is forever handing out candy and hugs no matter how rebellious the child is. It's true that God is love, but we have attempted to define love via humanistic insight, through our own lens and our own longings for acceptance. It's also true that God is longsuffering, but only He knows how long His suffering will be. The full force of His wrath will be released one day, and many lesser though terrible judgments will come before that happens. God is a fearful force to behold and we have been self-centred and entitled, presuming that approach will somehow draw us closer to His heart. God, Who is by definition love, will do what is necessary to preserve love".[35]

The serious condition Burton diagnoses is furthered by the "celebrity" culture of the ministry, both in preaching and music. Is God really gratified, much less honoured, by those who travel miles and miles to hear their favourite preacher and who buy expensive tickets to go and see a Christian gospel star lead worship, when all the while back home in the local church can't even drag themselves out of bed to worship on a Sunday morning? What has happened to us when personalities and fans have entered the vocabulary of Christian ministry and service? The church now hosts award ceremonies for ministry, and the record and reputations of many a Christian author and Bible teacher are listed on the covers of their books in a way that is alien for any servant of God according to the Scriptures. Only God is great. It has been well said, and better than I am trying to articulate it here, that we cannot be promoting self and parading our cleverness and, at the same time, presume we are glorifying God. "I am the LORD: that is my name: and my glory will I not give to another, neither my praise to graven images" (Isaiah 42:8 KJV).

How much of our lives is really intentionally considered as being for the glory of God when a lot of the time, over so much, we are talking about self and how we feel, who we are not happy with, why we are discontented, and what we are going to do about it, with little or no reference to God and what He says and wills? So obsessed with our little self-world of "Me, myself, I" while the rest of the world goes to hell. In one of my former pastorates, the comment of a parishioner was passed on to me: "I no longer feel as if this is my church anymore." My response was, "Good, now we're beginning to make some progress."

The Partnership of Separation

There are some beautiful, needful, and wonderful partnerships to be found, as Psalm 85 closes out: "Mercy and truth, met together … righteousness and peace, kissing … truth and righteousness, combining … righteousness/holiness setting the pace, leading the way" (KJV). Rev. Dr. Billy Graham commented, "Every revival that ever came in the history of the world, or in the history of the Church, laid great emphasis on the holiness of God."[36]

The holiness of God has significant consequences for us: holiness, "without which no man shall see the Lord" (Hebrews 12:14 KJV). Therefore, God sent Jesus, whom the Bible says is "the Lamb of God, which taketh away the sin of the world" (John 1:29 KJV). Jesus says, "Go, and sin no more" (John 8:11 KJV) – not "Go and sin less" or "in other more acceptable ways."

Only in Jesus Christ do "mercy and truth meet, righteousness and peace kiss, truth and righteousness combine" (NIV). Christ is always preceded by "righteousness." The "way of his steps" in the Incarnation was prepared by John the Baptist with a call to separation: "Repent ye: for the kingdom of heaven is at hand.... The voice of one crying in the wilderness, Prepare ye the way for the Lord, make his paths straight" (Matthew 3:1–3 KJV).

Not only have there been those down through church history who have tried to set Jesus and the apostle Paul against each other, but also Jesus and John the Baptist. Such is a futile exercise because it is a false distinction. We have already noted the message of John the Baptist. The Bible also tells us: "From that time Jesus began to preach, and to say, Repent: for the kingdom of heaven is at hand" (Matthew 4:17 KJV). Jesus says to His Disciples, "I tell you the truth; It is expedient for you that I go away: for if I go not away, the Comforter will not come unto you; but if I depart, I will send him unto you. And when he is come, he will reprove the world of sin, and of righteousness, and of judgment: Of sin, because they believe not on me; Of righteousness, because I go to my Father, and ye see me no more; Of judgment, because the prince of this world is judged" (John 16:7–11 KJV). In Acts 24:25, the Bible tells us that as Paul stood before Felix and Drusilla, he "reasoned of righteousness, temperance and judgment to come" (KJV).

There is a specific pattern to New Testament preaching which has been posted "missing in action" when it comes to much of the preaching from Western church pulpits today. To quote from Spurgeon again,

> "Repentance and forgiveness are joined together in the experience of all believers. There has never been a person yet who genuinely repented of sin that was not forgiven. On the other hand, no-one has ever been forgiven who had not repented of his sin. It is certain that in Heaven there are no cases of sin being washed away, unless at the same time the heart was led to repentance and faith in Christ. Hatred of sin and a sense of pardon come together into the soul and abide together while we live. These two things act and react upon each other. The man who is forgiven, repents; and the man who repents is most assuredly forgiven. You will never value pardon unless you feel repentance; and you will never taste the deepest draught of repentance until you know that you are pardoned".[37]

This is what happens when God comes. We have long lived in a day when so much emphasis is placed on the gifts of the Spirit to almost the exclusion of the character of the Holy Spirit and the life He is professed to live in: He is the Holy Spirit. In Acts 15:9, the one confirmation hell can neither mimic or manufacture, Peter used as proof that the Holy Spirit of God was present and working in the lives of Gentiles as well as Jews was not the possession and expression of any gift, but the evidence of a transformed life: "And put no difference between us and them, purifying their hearts by faith" (KJV). The partnership of separation taking place in the life of the believer cannot be overstated, underrated, or substituted.

Exhortation – Application = Frustration[38]

Whilst revivals at a national and local church level are neither as simple and ever-ready as Gypsy Smith's words might suggest, it is the case when it comes to personal revival. We can have a personal revival at any time we truly desire it and seek God for it. Indeed, the more personal revivals there are, how much more and directly and surely will revival be ushered in with the church and the nation?

O Holy Ghost, revival comes from Thee;
Send a revival, start the work in me;
Thy Word declares Thou wilt supply our need;
For blessings now, O Lord, I humbly plead.[39]

Jesus said in Luke 11:5–13 (NIV):

> Which of you shall have a friend, and shall go unto
> him at midnight, and say unto him, Friend, lend me

three loaves; For a friend of mine in his journey is come to me, and I have nothing to set before him? And he from within shall answer and say, Trouble me not: the door is now shut, and my children are with me in bed; I cannot rise and give thee. I say unto you, Though he will not rise and give him, because he is his friend, yet because of his importunity he will rise and give him as many as he needeth.

And I say unto you, Ask, and it shall be given you; seek, and ye shall find; knock, and it shall be opened unto you. For every one that asketh receiveth; and he that seeketh findeth; and to him that knocketh it shall be opened. If a son shall ask bread of any of you that is a father, will he give him a stone? or if he ask a fish, will he for a fish give him a serpent? Or if he shall ask an egg, will he offer him a scorpion? If ye then, being evil, know how to give good gifts unto your children: how much more shall your heavenly Father give the Holy Spirit to them that ask him?

Whilst God is "one pent up revival",[40] we must always be careful that we do not recklessly and rashly rush to apply these things in what we perceive to be revival.

A Scriptural Word of Caution

The wise preacher counsels, "It is not good to have zeal without knowledge, nor to be hasty and miss the way" (Proverbs 19:2 NIV). The apostle Paul described those who "have a zeal of God, but not according to knowledge" (Romans 10:2 KJV).

In their excellent book, *The Heart of a Great Pastor,* Neil Wiseman and H. B. London write:

> Today some churches toy, or even trifle, with revival. Like a small child….Magic quick-fix programs that cost little soul passion and require less commitment are sought.

> Sometimes, an entire congregation tries to make itself believe that a religious performance is an actual revival or that an overly energetic worship service is genuine revival. Performance, great crowds, and noise are not in themselves useful criteria. It is amazingly easy to fool ourselves into believing we are being renewed, when inside we are dried up.[41]

One of the clearest and costliest examples of this kind of pretence and presumption is recorded in the Bible in both Samuel and Chronicles. The Ark of the Covenant in the Old Testament was the greatest testimony of assurance to God's presence His people had. Foremost about the Ark was the holiness of God. God said, "If you touch it, you will die" (see Numbers 4:15). To prevent this, a certain group from the Levites, the Kohathites, were chosen to be responsible for handling and looking after "the most holy things" (Numbers 4:4 KJV) – not by touching them but by attaching poles to the "holy things."

There came a time later in Israel's history when the Ark of the Covenant was stolen by the Philistines. God allowed this because His people did not want to be separated from the world that they might be separated to Him. At the same time, they presumed on His unconditional protection of them. The Ark of the Covenant became too hot for the Philistines to handle, and they returned it to Israel, where it remained, in relative obscurity, at Abinadab's house (see 1

Samuel 4–7). After many years, having been established as king, David finally brought the Ark back to Jerusalem.

> They set the ark of God upon a new cart, and brought it out of the house of Abinadab that was in Gibeah: and Uzzah and Ahio, the sons of Abinadab, drave the new cart. And they brought it out of the house of Abinadab which was at Gibeah, accompanying the ark of God: and Ahio went before the ark.
>
> And David and all the house of Israel played before the LORD on all manner of instruments made of fir wood, even on harps, and on psalteries, and on timbrels, and on cornets, and on cymbals.
>
> And when they came to Nachon's threshingfloor, Uzzah put forth his hand to the ark of God, and took hold of it; for the oxen shook it. And the anger of the LORD was kindled against Uzzah; and God smote him there for his error; and there he died by the ark of God.
>
> (2 Samuel 6:3–7 KJV)

This was supposed to be a revival, marking a new, restored beginning with God for His people. Yet, consider what did happen, because of what had been ignored:

- a cart instead of poles
- celebration without consecration
- good intention but not strict obedience

The Ark would eventually get to Jerusalem, but not before David and the people had learned this terrible lesson. We read in 2 Samuel 6:13

(KJV): "And it was so, that when they that bare the ark of the LORD " – properly carried by poles on shoulders, not presumptuously pushed on carts.

The Chronicler records it (1 Chronicles 15:11–15 KJV):

> And David called for Zadok and Abiathar the priests, and for the Levites, for Uriel, Asaiah, and Joel, Shemaiah, and Eliel, and Amminadab, And said unto them, Ye are the chief of the fathers of the Levites: sanctify yourselves, both ye and your brethren, that ye may bring up the ark of the LORD God of Israel unto the place that I have prepared for it. For because ye did it not at the first, the LORD our God made a breach upon us, for that we sought him not after the due order. So the priests and the Levites sanctified themselves to bring up the ark of the LORD God of Israel. And the children of the Levites bare the ark of God upon their shoulders with the staves thereon, as Moses commanded according to the word of the LORD.

It happened – and happens – not because God is harsh, but because God is holy. Watchman Nee wrote,

> To the Israelites the ark of the Lord was the ark of His covenant. They fancied He would fulfil that covenant therefore by protecting them from their foes, no matter how untrue to it they themselves might be. But when God's children turn from Him with a divided heart He can only hand them over to defeat. They think He must deliver them for His glory's sake, but God is more concerned to vindicate His holy character than to display an empty show

of glory. When a servant of God fails badly, we feel
the affair were better covered up. We pray along
such lines therefore, expecting God, for His own
glory, to save from open shame, even though there
be secret defeat. But God's way is the very reverse
of this. He must let His people be defeated in the
world's eyes in order to dissociate Himself from
their unholiness. He will never cover it up. His glory
rests on moral values, and can be better maintained
by their open discomfiture than by the deception of
a hollow victory.[42]

God is still holy and still present. His holy presence is no longer fixed
on an Ark but in people like you and me: "But we have this treasure
in earthen vessels, that the excellency of the power may be of God,
and not of us" (2 Corinthians 4:7 NIV). We need to be careful with
His holy presence, continuing in and cleaving to "the due order" for
us the Bible is.

For too long, the holy presence of God has been pushed and
pulled around on the "carts" of our fleshly accommodation and
convenience. In too much there is celebration without consecration –
carnal "carts" instead of sanctified shoulders. Whether through
ignorance or defiance, the "due order" of God's Word has been
ignored by too many. The result? The "ark" – God's holy presence –
never gets to our Jerusalem in our day. God has never wanted our
well-meant intentions and good ideas ... just our obedience: "to obey
is better than sacrifice" (1 Samuel 15:22 KJV).

If you have read and stayed with this book to here – well done
and thank you. What do we do now? Where do we go? How
do we apply all this information and its appeal? If there is no
outworking, then we will become just like the Dead Sea. An old
Chinese proverb says:

"He who would take a thousand steps must take the first one."[43]

For too long and in too much the church has been living out its own version of "The Emperor's New Clothes"[44]: going along with flow of fantasy and the trend of novelty, whilst inwardly knowing that things are not truly as we are saying we are seeing and are professing to show. It is time to give up the charade, speak up over the truth, and look up to God as we live up to all He has made available to us in Christ.

"Go home....
Lock yourself in your room....
Kneel down in the middle of the floor and with a
piece of chalk, draw a circle round yourself....
There, on your knees, pray fervently and brokenly, that
God would start a Revival within that chalk circle!"[45]

(Gypsy Smith)

Conclusion

In 1904, the *Old Time Religion* published a timeless prayer for revival, as needfully relevant today as ever:

> *God, You are greatly in favour of Revival. You are now stirring up Your people to pray for what You desire. Our every other need sinks into insignificance compared to the need of a deep and widespread old time Revival....*

> *God, send us a Revival that will turn the people of God back from their worldliness and idols to serve the true and the living God - back from broken cisterns to the 'Fountain of living waters.'*

> *A Revival that will take away every desire for worldly amusements and abolish every ungodly scheme for raising money for the support of the Gospel.*

> *A Revival that will sweep away the pride that prompts all worldly conformity and extravagance in all dress and manner of life.*

A Revival that will take the people out of their worldly clubs and societies and secret lodges and put them in the 'secret place of the Most High where they will abide under the shadow of the Almighty.'

A Revival that will save the people of God from covetousness, the love of the world, and all uncleanness of spirit, mind and body.

A Revival in which professors of religion will have their eyes open to see and feel their responsibility for souls and in which they will confess with broken hearts their former backslidings, their carelessness and their indifference, and in thousands of cases, their actual transgressions of Your moral law.

A Revival like a flood that will 'sweep away the refuge of lies' and 'overthrow the hiding places' of all them that would hide away from the light of God's presence.

A Revival that will unearth and uncover every device of satan for deceiving souls, whether found in the Church or outside of it. 'For the secret of the Lord is with them that fear Him and He will show them His covenant.' (Psalm 25:14 KJV)

A Revival that will make both the Church and the world realise the shortness of time and the importance of eternity.

A Revival that will make Heaven and hell, Calvary and the resurrection, salvation from sin, cleansing through the blood and the gift of the Holy Spirit, living realities by the revelation of Your Spirit in harmony with the Word of God.

A Revival in which the sinfulness of sin will so be revealed that instead of excusing it and pleading for it, souls will turn from it in utter loathing and cry out, "O wretched man that I am, who shall deliver me from the body of this death?" (Romans 7:24 KJV)

A Revival that will sweep away all selfishness and narrowness and all sectarian spirit and bring those that now spend their time in criticism of each other down on their faces before God crying out for the salvation of lost souls.

A Revival like a tornado that will sweep away all the old dried-up sermons and all the cold formal prayers, and all the lifeless singing and like a whirlwind will carry everyone that comes in its path Heavenward.

A Revival that will fill the hearts of saints with holy love, and so burden the hearts of God's ministers, that the Word of God will be like fire shut up in their bones.

A Revival that will help the people honour God with their substance, and have their barns filled with plenty.

A Revival that has so much of Heaven and so much of God's glory in it that all the world will be compelled to see and feel its mighty influence.

A Revival that will gloriously defeat the powers of darkness and hell, and make earth and Heaven ring with shouts of victory over a multitude of souls snatched from eternal burnings, and run for God and Heaven.

Yes, a Revival that will never need to be revived! But that will sweep on like a mighty wave of the sea that nothing can hinder, until time shall be no more.

For such a Revival, O God we pray![46]

Amen and Amen!

To Whom It May Concern

A concerned husband went to the family doctor to talk about his wife. He said, "Doctor, I think my wife is deaf because she never hears me the first time and always asks me to repeat things."

"Well," the doctor replied, "go home and tonight stand about fifteen feet from her and say something to her. If she doesn't reply, move about five feet closer and say it again. Keep doing this so that we'll get an idea about the level of her deafness."

With that instruction, the husband went home and put it to work. He began by standing the prescribed fifteen feet from his wife, who was in the kitchen chopping some vegetables. "Darling," he said, "what's for dinner?"

No response.

The husband then moved about five feet closer and again asks the question ... still no reply.

He moved another five feet closer ... no reply.

Finally, the exasperated husband gets right behind his unsuspecting wife, about an inch away, and shouts, "Darling, what's for dinner?"

She replies, "For the fourth time, vegetable soup!"

No one has the monopoly on hearing. Lapses in listening happen to many and can befall any. In both the gospel accounts and Revelation of Jesus Christ, the Bible, more than once, records Jesus saying, even pleading, "He that hath ears to hear, let him hear" (Matthew 11:15, 13:9, 43; Mark 4:9, 23; Luke 8:8, 14:35; Revelation 2–3 KJV). We all need, and would do well, to heed His plea.

A Plea for Biblical Authority

"Preach the word; be instant in season, out of season; reprove, rebuke, exhort with all longsuffering and doctrine" (2 Timothy 4:2 KJV).

The Bible is the only source and measure of truth and hope and life. To "edit" God's Book has been rightly likened to a postal worker tampering with our personal mail. As the only remaining prophets of today – who "forth-tell" the written Word, *not* fore-tell, and fairy-tale another word – God's preachers are not called upon to be political commentators, emotional counsellors, court jesters, or novelty conjurers of the always new. The Bible is the inspired Word of God. With the conclusion and closing of the Scriptural canon, this divine inspiration of inerrancy ceased, as did any new revelation beyond the Bible. Illumination, by consequence of our necessity, is always going on, Lord willing, in increasing measure in us. The need is not for a further Word but for us to go deeper into the Word that already is.

"Is there any word from the LORD?" (Jeremiah 37:17 KJV) King Zedekiah's question to the prophet Jeremiah is still being uttered by many in the darkness of a troubled mind and seeking heart, even in the fallout of foolish choices. It is a need-filled question, and the answer it anticipates, because of the direction it looks to and listens in, should bring a worthy answer. In a world of anarchy – even within our Churches – how we need to hear words of authority.

A Plea for Gospel Clarity

"Woe is unto me, if I preach not the gospel!" (1 Corinthians 9:16 KJV)

If and when asked, many of the Christ-ones in our local Churches will not be able to remember the last time they heard a gospel sermon preached; we have remained evangelical in what we believe but are no longer evangelistic in how we reach. There is a generation of Church people who have never heard any teaching on "righteousness, temperance, and judgment to come" (Acts 24:25 KJV) as the apostle Paul would have presented. When did sin, hell, Church discipline, and tithing – to name but a few – drop out of our vocabulary because they had been eliminated from our doctrine and practice?

Jesus Christ is *not* a

- problem solver,
- life enhancer,
- career builder,
- cash dispenser, or
- doting grandfather.

Christ *is* the

- soul saver,
- truth teller,
- disciple maker,
- Son conformer, and
- God Revealer.

There is still a heaven to gain and a hell to shun. Our need is not to be proved right but to be made right, in the forgiveness of sins and a cleansed heart. We cannot sing ourselves, buy ourselves, or positively confess and think ourselves better and clean in the sight of a holy God. We need a Saviour and Sanctifier: "This is a faithful saying, and worthy of all acceptation, that Christ Jesus came into the world to save sinners" (1 Timothy 1:15 KJV).

A Plea for Personal Integrity

"Take heed unto thyself, and unto the doctrine" (1 Timothy 4:16 KJV).

Second only to being called "Mum" or "Dad," the highest honour-of-trust in all the world is to have someone call you "Pastor," as you are given permission to see them at their very worst and best, and at many other points and places in between. I believe that with all my heart and for the last twenty-six years have had the privilege of being in this trusted position. If this is not enough, add to it the wonder-filled responsibility of being able to open God's Book to people; it is the best job going. Why would you swap it, leave it, or forfeit it for anything?

One of the consequences of all the above is the influence we have to help and hinder. How much hurt has been visited upon trusting people and grief caused to the Holy Spirit when we do not live out ourselves what we proclaim and profess to be before others? We rightly acknowledge that some of the pressures and expectations thrust on pastors and preachers are unfair because they are unrealistic; however, it is not wrong to ask them to live up to any expectation, especially when what is being asked for is some gut-level honesty and genuine humility, in a faith that lives every day, not needing to lie on Sundays, by the grace of God.

> The law of the LORD is perfect, converting the soul: the testimony of the LORD is sure, making wise the simple.

The statutes of the LORD are right, rejoicing the heart: the commandment of the LORD is pure, enlightening the eyes.

The fear of the LORD is clean, enduring for ever: the judgments of the LORD are true and righteous altogether.

More to be desired are they than gold, yea, than much fine gold: sweeter also than honey and the honeycomb.

Moreover by them is Thy servant warned: and in keeping of them there is great reward.

Who can understand His errors? cleanse thou me from secret faults.

Keep back Thy servant also from presumptuous sins; let them not have dominion over me: then shall I be upright, and I shall be innocent from the great transgression.

Let the words of my mouth, and the meditation of my heart, be acceptable in Thy sight, O LORD, my Strength, and my Redeemer.

(Psalm 19:7–14 KJV)

Notes

1. Realisation

1   J. Edwin Orr, *The Church Must First Repent: Chapters on Revival* (Marshall Morgan & Scott, 1937)

2   Ibid.

3   C.H. Spurgeon, *Feeding Sheep or Amusing Goats* (Posted and quoted by many, unable to identify original source)

2. Declaration

4   Ronald F. Youngblood, *N.I.V. Study Bible* (Zondervan, Grand Rapids, Michigan, 2011)

5   Leonard Ravenhill (Source Unknown)

6   Paul Rees (Source Unknown)

7   A.W. Tozer, *The Radical Cross: Living the Passion of Christ* (Moody Publishers, 2009)

8   Pastor Gary Gilley, taken from *The False Gospel Of...* seminar posted on YouTube

9 Wilbur Smith (Source Unknown)

10 A.W. Tozer, *Keys to the Deeper Life* (Zondervan, 1957, 1988)

11 Charles Finney, *How to Promote a Revival* (Lectures on Revivals of Religion, 1868)

12 David F. Wells, *Losing Our Virtue: Why The Church Must Recover Its Moral Vision* (Grand Rapids: Eerdmans, 1998)

13 Rev. John Paton (Letter to Pastors from Nazarene District Superintendent, used with permission)

14 Leonard Ravenhill, *Why Revival Tarries* (Sovereign World, 1992 British Edition)

15 Bessie Porter Head, "O Breath of Life, Come Sweeping Through Us" (1920, Public Domain)

3. Desperation

16 Jim Cymbala, *Fresh Wind, Fresh Fire* (Zondervan Publishing House, 1997)

17 Keith Green, "Asleep in the Light" (Warner/Chappell Music, Inc., Universal Music Publishing Group)

18 William Shakespeare, *Julius Caesar*, Act I, Scene III, L.140-141

19 Leonard Ravenhill, *Why Revival Tarries* (Sovereign World, 1992 British Edition)

20 General Dwight Eisenhower (Source Unknown)

21 Pastor Martin Rinkhart (1586-1649), "Now Thank We All Our God" (Public Domain)

22 Pastor Randall Denney (Sermon on Jude)

23 Bakht Singh, in *Conquest for Christ*, the official organ of International Students, Inc.

24 Jonathan Goforth, *By My Spirit* (Grand Rapids, Michigan: Zondervan Publishing House, 1942)

4. Separation

25 Dr. Paul Tournier, *To Understand Each Other* (Westminster John Knox Press, 1967)

26 Posted and quoted by many, unable to identify original source

27 Katharina Von Schlegel (1697-?), "Be Still, My Soul"

28 Leonard Ravenhill (Unknown Source)

29 Anonymous

30 Charles Finney, *Death to Sin Through Christ* (Printed in *The Oberlin Evangelist*, 14 September 1853)

31 A.W. Tozer, *Knowledge of the Holy* (Authentic Media, 2005, 1961)

32 Ibid.

33 David Wilkerson (Source Unknown)

34 John Burton, *Is It Time For Hell Fire Preaching Again?* (in *Charisma News*, July 2015, Charisma Media)

35 Ibid.

36 Rev. Dr. Billy Graham, quoted by Hanspeter Nüesch, *Ruth and Billy Graham: The Legacy of A Couple* (Baker Books, 2014)

37 C.H. Spurgeon, *All of Grace* (Moody Classics, Moody Press, 1974, 1885)

5. Application

Conclusion

Pervaded by the stench of self-satisfaction, self-obsession, and self-justification, the Church in the West, overcome by its culture, finds herself in an ailing condition very few seem to want to mention, never mind confront to correct. Biblical imperatives often go unheeded in the pew, largely because they are unsounded from the pulpit, as we live out our own dark and more sinister version of "The Emperor's New Clothes."

Drawing primarily from the Scriptures, along with other revival writers such as Finney, Tozer, Ravenhill, *Getting Ready for Revival!* seeks to stimulate our minds out of our ignorance of God's Word and stir our hearts over our forgetfulness of God, returning us to the living "wells" (Deuteronomy 6:10–12), not of our own making or sustaining, but of God's provision and insistence that we may not die in such graves of our own.

About the Author

Stuart D. Reynolds was born in Scotland and trained for the ministry at the Nazarene Theological College in Manchester, England. He has pastored churches in Scotland, England, and Northern Ireland. He and his wife, Helen, have two daughters, Heather and Leah. At present, Stuart is in itinerant evangelism and revivalism in the U.K. and United States under the auspices of "Ears to Hear Ministries."

Stuart has recorded five albums: "Filled with Your Love," "Stay with Me," "One More Song," "On the Other Side," and "Simple Faith." He has also written *The Broken Pastor.*

Stuart and Helen now live in England.

If you would like to book Stuart for a meeting, conference, concert, or any other event, he can be contacted through email, at:

reynolds.stuart1@sky.com,
http://sdhareynolds.wixsite.com/earstohearministries
or mobile (+44) 07816 853 551
or home (+44) (0)1623 367 758.

Also By Stuart D Reynolds

The Broken Pastor
The voice of a pastor for the ear of the church

So many pastors are hurting, seeming to be constantly on the verge of quitting, feeling like failures, having the last embers of self-worth kicked and stomped out of them, having the added burdens of guilt in themselves and censure from their denominations if they were to ever admit to and express these things. No matter the identity of pastor, location, or church, for the pastor, in particular, who reads, it is himself he is reading about, where he is, how he is broken. This book is not only for pastors – broken or otherwise. It is the prayer-filled hope and working intention of the writer that also reading these words will be church board members along with the wider congregation. This is a book for the whole church, In a world where broken things are not so much fixed as rubbished and discarded, no longer regarded as being useful, *The Broken Pastor* still works.

ISBN 978 1935507 352

Printed in the United States
By Bookmasters